All color book of
Wine
by David Milligan

Octopus Books

Contents

An Introduction
to drinking wine
4

Vineyards round
the world
10

The vintage,
production & bottling
of wine
24

Table wines & the
great first growths
36

Champagne and
sparkling wines
59

Fortified wines
66

Acknowledgements
72

First published 1974 by
Octopus Books Limited
59 Grosvenor Street, London W1

ISBN 0 7064 0293 6

© 1974 Octopus Books Limited

Distributed in USA by Crescent Books
a division of Crown Publishers Inc
419 Park Avenue South, New York NY10016

Distributed in Australia by Rigby Limited
30 North Terrace, Kent Town
Adelaide, South Australia 5067

Produced by Mandarin Publishers Limited
14 Westlands Road, Quarry Bay, Hong Kong

Printed in Hong Kong

An Introduction to drinking wine

Drinking wine can either be a very simple pleasure or a very complex subject according to the individual. There is nothing simpler or less demanding than the casual acceptance and every day enjoyment of wine in wine-producing countries, where a carafe of wine is a more regular feature on the dinner table than a jug of water. Equally, for the wine enthusiast, there is no end to the knowledge of wine to be gained and the complexities to be unravelled. Each individual row of vines in every vineyard and also each vintage produces a subtly different wine and provides ample scope for the connoisseur's comparison and deliberation.

Today, for several reasons, an ever increasing range of wines from every corner of the world is available to the consumer, and there is a much greater selection now than there was normally available to our grandparents. One of the most important reasons for this is the technical improvement in the making and bottling of wines, which now permits even those that are very delicate to be shipped successfully around the world. There are in fact very few wines today which cannot 'travel' successfully if handled properly. Another reason is that the enormous increase in the worldwide wine consumption has meant that traditional areas can no longer supply the world's needs and the professional wine buyer must seek new sources from which to satisfy the demands of his clientèle.

Finally, this very increase in demand means that under that oldest of economic laws — supply and demand — wines from the traditional, classic wine-producing areas have risen so sharply in price that they are beyond the reach of many except for special occasions.

This great diversity adds another interest for the true wine lover — that is constantly to search out the best value for money amongst the many new and often unfamiliar wines that are available to him. Indeed, it is certain that many completely new areas will be planted with vines in the near future, as the vine can produce successfully given suitable soil conditions in any temperate climate.

In the northern hemisphere, the most northerly vineyards are found in the Champagne country of France and Germany and stretch as far south as the vineyards of Tunisia, Morocco and Algeria. In the southern hemisphere, there are many vineyards in Argentina and Chile, as well as in South Africa, Australia and New Zealand.

We do not know when wine was first produced, but the earliest vines seem to have been in the Middle East, and there are references to vines in ancient writings and cave paintings. Remains in some of the Egyptian tombs seem to indicate wine being used for funeral purposes as early as 3000 BC. Around 2000 BC, in ancient Babylon, there were laws governing the sale of wine and certainly, by the time of the Greek Empire, a thousand years before Christ, wine was already an important factor and vines were carried by the Greeks and others to Italy, Spain,

Southern France and North Africa where they were planted for the first time.

Wine was probably first discovered by accident when a bunch of grapes with burst skins was left for a period so that the juices ran out and the wild yeast on the skins acted on these juices to cause a fermentation. No doubt someone poured off the resultant liquid, tasted it, liked it, possibly enjoying a mildly pleasant sensation from the alcohol. However and wherever it was discovered, the development of wine growing and wine making has been steady with only a few occasional setbacks. For instance the Emperor Domitian in Roman times, in order to protect the Italian vineyards, ordered many areas throughout the empire to uproot their vines. The most recent parallel was when, after the Franco-Prussian war, the vineyards of Alsace were planted in inferior varieties in order not to compete with the German wines. Over the years, the wine growers in the different regions have found the vines best suited to their soil and the type of wine that they wished to produce. Scientists and horticulturists have produced many new varieties of vine suited to special climates by crossing existing varieties.

The technology of the actual process of wine making has improved dramatically. The handling of the grapes from the moment of picking to the final bottling and storage of the wine is now much speedier and more efficient. The value of cleanliness and sterility was discovered and also of careful selection and ageing at all the different stages of production, so that today any well made wine can be shipped successfully to any point on the globe using the latest methods of shipment under controlled temperatures.

The Cultivation of the Vine

In addition to having a suitable composition of soil, the situation of the vineyard is important. The best vineyards are generally found on slopes facing south so that there is maximum exposure to the sun. The slope is important as it helps to drain the vineyard and also equally important, affords a measure of protection from frost, as frost forms only in still air conditions which occur more frequently in depressions of the ground in the plains.

Once these factors have been determined, the choice of the vine is extremely important. In many areas of the world, particularly in France, government regulations will stipulate the permitted varieties of vine that may be planted in order to produce a particular named wine. In many areas, such as Bordeaux, a vineyard will be planted with several different varieties which, when blended together in the final wine, give the character sought for that particular district.

It must be remembered that four years will elapse from the planting of the vine to the first production of grapes suitable for wine making, and six years before the vine is producing a reasonable quantity of good quality wine. Most vines today are the result of grafting native varieties onto American root stocks. This practice started at the end of the last century after the dreaded Phylloxera louse, which had been brought to Europe accidentally with some experimental vines from the United States, spread all over Europe and over a period of some thirty years completely devastated its vineyards. Curious as it may seem, it was found that though Phylloxera originated with vines bought from the United States, it was found that the American vine roots themselves were resistant to this louse.

The labours of the vineyard are many and arduous. They commence following the vintage with the cleaning up of the vineyards after the leaves have fallen. The vine roots are then protected to some extent from the winter weather by the piling up around them of the earth from between each row, which also assists the drainage of winter rains.

When winter ends, the vines are pruned. This is a most important and skilled operation that affects not only the quality of the wine for that year but also the future crops, as incorrect pruning or selection of shoots can considerably damage the vine's production in future years.

The work of pruning lasts for two or three months and once the danger of severe frosts is ended the earth is removed once again from around the roots of the vines. In March the *vigneron* sees to the ploughing of the vineyard to break up and aerate the soil between the rows.

At the same time, the sap begins to rise in the vines and around April is the time to plant out new vine cuttings in sections of the vineyard that are being replanted. Most experienced vineyard owners try to replace a certain number of older vines each year in order to maintain a balance of age throughout the vineyard. During the spring and summer there is much work to be done in spraying the vines against attacks of various different diseases and according to the weather conditions each year as many as seven or eight sprayings may be necessary.

A critical period is when the vines flower, generally during the early part of June. Throughout the summer the weather conditions are supremely important; good weather in June ensures undamaged flowers and successful pollination which will set the scene for a good quality and plentiful vintage, whereas rain or heavy winds can do a great deal of damage. It is generally calculated that the vintage will begin 100 days from the commencement of the flowering. During this period, a delicate balance of sunshine to ripen the grapes and rain to keep them full of juice is necessary, but prolonged periods of either can cause the *vigneron* concern. According to the area, the vintage (in the Northern hemisphere) will occur any time after the middle of September and may continue as late as November or December in the Northern parts of Europe, such as Germany.

The Vintage and the Making of the Wine

The vintage, which is the culmination of the *vigneron's* work takes place in the autumn. The grapes are gathered by casual labourers who arrive especially for this task. It is extremely hard work and the pickers begin around eight in the morning and in most vineyards will continue picking until six in the evening. The system generally used is for a group to go in to a particular section of the vineyard with small baskets into which they put the freshly cut bunches. These are then collected by workers carrying larger baskets on their backs who will carry these to waiting tractors with even larger containers, which will transport the grapes to the winery and then return for another load.

Exactly when to start picking is one of the most important and difficult judgements the *vigneron* has to make. In periods of fine weather each day of delay can considerably improve the quality of the wine and hence the eventual price it will fetch. On the other hand, the later the vintage, the more likelihood there is of being caught by rain or even sometimes an early frost, and if it rains, the quality of the wine made from the wet grapes will be worse than that which would have resulted from an early picking. This decision of the vineyard owner is one that is aided by years of experience and by the more reliable advance weather forecasts of recent years. It is nevertheless an anxious moment for the growers and once the picking commences it is conducted with all speed.

In certain areas, notably the United States, experiments have been made with mechanical picking of the grapes which appear to be very successful. They do however require that the vines be planted further apart than usual, in order to allow the machines to pass between the rows. One particular experiment even involves pressing and crushing the grapes in the vineyard and transferring the juice to tankers running alongside the picking machines. However, these methods are only suited to large scale operations and the hand pickers will be with us for many years to come.

The principles of wine making are very simple, being based on the action of yeast on the sugar in the juice which causes fermentation. This means the sugar is converted into alcohol, giving off carbon dioxide gas as a by product. However, the skill of the wine maker and the quality of his equipment is of enormous importance as the same grapes treated by two different people under different conditions will produce distinctly different wines.

When the grapes arrive at the winery they are first put through a machine which removes the stalks from the bunches. The red grapes will then be put through a crusher which breaks their skins. The resultant mixture of juice and skins is pumped to a fermenting vat where it is allowed to remain in most cases for upwards of seven days. The small film of wild yeast which is on the skin of those grapes is all that is needed to start fermentation, though increasingly, particularly in the western hemisphere, selected strains of yeast are used and the original yeasts are eliminated.

After fermentation, the wine is run off into barrels or vats for further ageing and development. The residue of skins and pulp is then pressed in a hydraulic press. This pressed wine is normally kept separate from the free run juice and in the better vineyards would not be sold under the vineyard name but would be reserved for consumption by the vineyard workers or the household.

The white grapes normally go straight from the stem-crusher to the press and from there they will go straight into a fermenting vat. It is possible to make white wine from red grapes and this is done by separating the juice at the time of pressing so that it has no chance to pick up colouring from the pigmentation of the skins. Rosé wines are treated like red wines except that the juice is separated from the skin after only a few hours, as soon as it has picked up the amount of colour desired.

Fortified wines are those that have alcohol added to bring them up to a high strength and stability, and there are two main groups: Sherry and Port. Sherry is made by the addition of a

predetermined amount of brandy after fermentation of the wine is complete and all the sugar has disappeared. Less is added for the dryer sherries and more for richer cream sherries. In the case of port, the brandy is added during the latter part of the fermentation before all the sugar has been fermented and this accounts for the luscious, sweet flavour of most ports.

There are several methods of making sparkling wines. The classic method is that of the Champagne district of France, where in the spring following the vintage, wines from different parts of the Champagne district are blended to give the special flavour of a particular Champagne firm. They are then rebottled with the addition of a small amount of yeast and sugar sufficient to cause a second fermentation in the bottle. One of the by-products of this fermentation is carbon dioxide gas which, as it cannot escape from the bottle, is retained and forms the sparkle or bubbles in the wine. The other by-product is the dead yeast cells, which, having completed their task fall to the bottom of the bottle to form a very fine sediment.

In order to remove this sediment from the wine without causing it to lose its sparkle, the bottles are put through an elaborate process by highly skilled workmen. The necks of the bottles are placed in a horizontal position in small holes in wooden frame racks and shaken each day in a special fashion. The workmen gradually transfer the bottles from a horizontal to a vertical position with the neck downwards, at the same time working all the sediment down to the neck of the bottle where it forms a small mound on the cork. This process can take as long as three months with workmen riddling the bottles every couple of days.

After this, and after a period of ageing when the bottles are stored in the vertical position, they are then passed along a conveyor with the first half inch or inch of the neck submerged in a freezing solution. This has the effect of freezing the sediment inside pellets of wine about one half inch above the cork. The bottles are turned the right way up and the cork is removed. The pellet flies out taking the sediment with it and the bottle is then quickly put on a machine which adds a measured amount of sweetening wine and then as much pure champagne as is needed to refill the bottle. It also recorks the bottle.

Different people have different tastes of sweetness and it is the practice in Champagne to add a greater or lesser amount of sweetening wine to each bottle prior to shipment. The driest of the Champagnes (and also the rarest) is the Champagne Natur to which no sugar has been added, the next driest is Brut with a minute addition of sweetening wine and finally, extra dry and demi-sec, each progressively sweeter.

This brief summary of the process of making champagne in France gives some indication of the enormous amount of manual labour involved. It is however, possible to produce

sparkling wines less expensively by conducting the second fermentation in a large vat and then filtering the wine under pressure prior to bottling. This is the method largely used for making sparkling wine in the United States and many countries outside France. It produces a pleasant wine, but one which does not match French Champagne in flavour nor in the quality of its bubbles, or *mousse*, as the French call it.

There is an intermediate process between the French and the Bulk process or Charmat method, as the fermentation in the tank is called, and that is the transfer process whereby the second fermentation takes place in the bottle as in the French process and then following the fermentation the bottle is decanted under pressure. The wine is filtered and then re-bottled. This method has some of the advantages of both the two previously described methods and seems to be most satisfactory for mass consumption sparkling wines.

In a few places, fortunately very few, sparkling wine is made by direct addition of CO_2 to the wine at the time of bottling. The characteristic of these wines is that the sparkle disappears almost as soon as the wine is poured.

Maturation

Table wines are usually bottled after six months to two years in barrels or in vat. Then begins the period of maturation in the bottle. One of the greatest problems for amateurs and professionals alike is to estimate correctly from a label or wine list whether a particular wine has reached its peak of maturity and when would be the ideal time to drink it.

In general, the more expensive the wine when it is first made, the longer it should be kept and the more likely it is to improve and develop in flavour with age. There are, however, many variables which affect the development and ageing of the wine. The most general rules are that white wines and very light red wines such as Beaujolais should be drunk within four years, and that heavier red wines can be drunk from upwards of three years after the vintage. In general, great white wine of a good year should last at least ten years. Some examples are the white burgundies such as Le Montrachet and Corton Charlemagne, and white Bordeaux such as Château D'Yquem and the great Auslese and Beerenauslese from Germany. A good year is basically one when the weather conditions are ideal for cultivating the grapes and for the vintage prevailing. Grapes that are fully ripe at the time of the vintage produce the highest quality wine.

Amongst the reds of good years, the great red Burgundies such as Richebourg, Chambertin and Romanée Conti should last fifteen years without difficulty and the fine clarets of Bordeaux are the longest lasting of all. Any of the top classified growths (first to fifth of the Medoc and the *grand crus* of St Emilion, Pomerol and Graves) will last ten years at least. The very top growths such as Château Lafite, Château Mouton-Rothschild,

This magnificent view of the vineyards of St Emilion is taken from Château Ausone, which together with Château Cheval Blanc was classified as one of the two great growths of St Emilion. The wines of St Emilion were not included in the 1855 classification of the Medoc Châteaux. They fall into two main groups: those from the gravelly soil of the plateau that adjoins the Pomerol district, and those of the slopes that we see here where the plateau ends in the town of St Emilion itself and the vineyards flow down the slopes into the plain beneath. The rock is not far below the surface here and the cellars of Château Ausone were carved from the rock. The Château is named after the Roman poet Ausonius who made his home here, and mentioned the excellent wine in his writings.

		1971	*1970*	1969	1967	*1966*	1964	*1961*	*1961*	*1959*
Red Bordeaux		1971	*1970*	1969	1967	*1966*	1964	*1961*	*1961*	*1959*
White Bordeaux	Sweet		*1970*	1969	1967	1966	*1962*	*1961*	1959	
	Dry		*1970*	1969	*1967*	1966	*1964*	1962		
Red Burgundy		1971	*1970*	*1969*	1967	*1966*	1964	1962	*1961*	*1959*
White Burgundy		1971	*1970*	*1969*	1967	*1966*	1964	*1962*	1961	
Rhine		*1971*	1970	1969	*1967*	*1966*	1964			
Moselle/Saar		*1971*	1970	*1969*	1967	1966	*1964*			
Alsace		*1971*	1970	*1969*	*1967*	1966	*1964*	1961		
California	White	*1971*	*1970*	1969	*1968*	1967	*1966*	1965	1964	
(Napa Valley)	Red	1971	*1970*	1969	*1968*	1967	*1966*	1965	1964	

Château Latour and Château Cheval Blanc may need as much as twenty years to reach their peak. Rosé wines should be drunk very young, preferably within a year or two of the vintage in order to appreciate their youthful freshness.

There are, of course, exceptions to most statements about wine and even the better wines from lesser years, whether red or white, are generally best drunk no more than five to six years after the vintage. Generalization is always difficult as even within a quite small region marked climatic differences can occur and the skill or lack of skill of the individual vintner can make considerable difference in the quality produced in good and bad years. However, the advanced technology in recent years has done a lot to improve the overall quality of wine made. Bad years are undoubtedly not as bad as they used to be. Finally, in England and the United States the consumer is well protected by several stages of selection and very few 'off' vintages are shipped to either country.

Any wines that are imported in an 'off' year are generally the exceptions that have succeeded in making a good wine. For this reason, knowledge of vintages no longer deserves the importance it formerly had and it has never been a major factor with American wines due to the much more stable climatic conditions in the American vineyards. The connoisseur and buyer of fine wines will always have access to enough information to enable him to seek out the best. A listing of the best recent vintages by region is given above (very good years in italics).

The Buying of Wine

When buying for home use, the choice of the place where one buys wine is almost as important, in some cases, as the actual wine selected. For less expensive everyday wines, the super-market or grocery store can be a satisfactory source. For better wines they are not such a good bet, as all the wines are normally stored standing up and if they do not have much demand for good wines, the chances are the bottle may have been there for some time. However, for the more adventurous customer, this can be a challenge, as the wines offered are sometimes mispriced and great bargains are sometimes to be found among the more expensive wines.

However, it is in the area of better wines that the specialist wine store comes into its own. Here, you should be able to obtain advice and information about all the different wines on sale, something that you certainly do not find at the super-market and the proprietor will generally have carefully selected the wines in his store for their value and quality.

It is always worth making a friend out of the owner of your wine store. Once he realizes that you are interested and you have been able to give him some idea of your tastes, perhaps by a trial purchase of several different types that he has recommended, he will then be in a position to know the types of wine that you like and make recommendations according to your taste. He can also tell you which vintages are the best buy, how long they will last and for those who are interested in building up a stock of wine at home he can advise which wines will appreciate most in value. He can also warn you about which wines are becoming scarce and that should therefore be bought before they disappear from the market.

Reading wine labels is somewhat confusing until the system is understood, when it will be found that most wine labels are very informative. They state the type of wine and the particular area or vineyard from which it comes, the name of the man who made it, the name of the exporter and importer, as well as the year in which the wine was made.

The best way to learn how to buy good wines is to record carefully your opinion of each wine that you taste and this will enable you to begin to develop a list of the producers and shippers whose wines you generally enjoy and find to be good value. You will then be able to seek out those in the future.

Buying wines in restaurants is a different matter as the choice is generally less wide and prices are, of course, higher due to the restaurant's overhead and cost of service. This is why knowledge of your favourite producer or shipper is useful and good restaurants should include this information on their wine lists. If they do not, you can always ask. The best values on restaurant wine lists, due to their methods of pricing, are generally in the middle to more expensive price ranges which is where you will find, as a rule, the better French wines. The overall quality of a restaurant can often be judged by the attention given to the presentation and service of its wines, as a fine restaurant realizes that wine is an important part of the complete experience of dining and will therefore give it the attention that it deserves.

The Wine Cellar

The correct storage of wine after it has been bought is very important if one is to get the most from a wine.

Wine cellars in the producing countries of Europe are generally around 13°C, but satisfactory storage can be obtained in a constant temperature that is maintained anywhere between 10°C and 21°C. It is, however, important to avoid constant or violent fluctuation of the temperature even within this range as this can cause cloudiness or deposit in a wine.

Wine should always be protected from direct light and vibration. Bottles should always be stored lying on their sides, since this ensures that the cork is kept damp and slightly swollen, thus maintaining the perfect seal, as exposure to the air can cause wine to turn to vinegar.

A most important article in the wine cellar is the cellar book in which details of all wines bought for maturing should be kept. It is useful but not essential for wines bought for everyday consumption. The following information should be recorded: date of purchase, full description of the wine, vintage, name of shipper and importer, where purchased, price and quantity. Additional space should be left to record the withdrawal of bottles and the remaining balance, as well as tasting notes which are useful in deciding when to serve the next bottle.

Serving of Wine

The correct service of wine adds greatly to the full enjoyment of a bottle and also the value obtained from it. White wines are the easiest to serve since they do not normally contain any sediment and merely require chilling to 7°C-10°C. This takes about an hour in a refrigerator or ten to twenty minutes in an ice bucket. Due to the close contact with the bottle and the faster melting of the ice, a mixture of ice and water chills faster and more effectively than ice alone. Rosé wines require the same treatment as white wine.

Younger red wines do not have any sediment and should be stored at about 16°C-18°C for at least an hour or so before serving and will benefit from the cork being drawn at the same time. This allows oxygen to come into contact with the wine and release the volatile elements that produce much of the aroma and taste of wine. Light red wines such as Beaujolais are

often more agreeable even cooler at a temperature of around 14°C.

Some older Red Bordeaux and Burgundies especially may have a slight sediment, but if the bottle is allowed to stand upright for two to three days before serving and the cork is carefully withdrawn an hour before, there will be no problem. The wine should be poured steadily and the last half inch of the wine allowed to stay in the bottle. The sediment is formed of tannin and natural colouring matter whose precipitation is part of the normal process of maturation.

For a very old wine with a heavy sediment, there are two approaches. One involves standing the bottle up where possible for about two weeks or more before serving and then after drawing the cork, pouring it carefully into a clean decanter. For this it is necessary to have a steady hand and a bright light against which to check the progress of the sediment towards the neck of the bottle whilst decanting. It is important to stop pouring once the sediment reaches the neck as even a small amount of sediment gives an unpleasant, bitter taste to the wine.

The second method of dealing with an old wine with a heavy sediment is the use of a decanting basket. The bottle is transferred from its horizontal storage position into a basket which holds it at about a 20 degree angle from horizontal. In this way, the wine can be brought gently to the table and uncorked. When serving, the whole bottle should be served at the first pouring except for the last half inch which will contain the sediment.

A clear, crystal decanter shows off the colour of the wine well and is a decorative addition to a dinner table. To show wine at its best, clear glasses of at least 6 oz. capacity are desirable. They should be designed to taper at the top in order to concentrate the aroma. For the same reason, these glasses should not be filled more than half to two-thirds full.

The Choice of Wine

The choice of the wine for the occasion depends on the taste of the individual, but nevertheless, over the years certain combinations have proved successful in pleasing the taste of many, and I have listed a selection of these.

Today the wine lover does not necessarily foreswear spirits entirely but most people agree that a spirit drink before a meal does somewhat deaden the palate and the appreciation of the meal when it finally arrives.

Aperitifs (and wine for occasions without food)
There is a wide range to choose from. Sherries, especially the dry ones, are old favourites. Madeira is also making a return. There is growing favour for the sweeter wine based aperitifs such as Dubonnet. That old Burgundian favourite, Kir, a mixture of five parts dry white burgundy to one part Crème de Cassis (blackcurrant cordial) can also be made with dry vermouth. Vermouth itself, on the rocks, either straight of half sweet and half dry, is also becoming more popular. Many people today are now serving a cool glass of white wine, pure and simple. A dry white burgundy or light refreshing Moselle, with its hint of sweetness, are most appropriate.

The classic aperitif of all is Champagne and this, for many, is the best choice.

Soups
If a wine is to be served, a medium dry sherry or Madeira is the

This Pinot Noir vine is seen just before the vintage and is in extremely good condition supporting several large, healthy bunches. Pinot Noir is the main grape planted in Burgundy and also, strangely enough, in Champagne where many brands are made from as much as 80 per cent Pinot Noir grapes. The vine is also much prized for producing the varietal wines in California. *Varietal* is the word used to describe wines made from at least 51 per cent of one grape variety, and most wineries in fact use one grape exclusively to a much greater extent than that. These varietal wines are considered to be the best of the table wines produced in California.

most appropriate and a little poured in the soup during its preparation will generally improve the flavour.

Hors d'oeuvres, fish dishes, white meat and eggs

This is the realm of white wines and the precise choice will depend as much on the method of cooking as much as anything else. Personal taste can decide between the drier white burgundies and Alsatian wines and the slightly sweeter German wines. A plainly cooked dish will call for a lighter wine whereas a well seasoned dish or one with a rich sauce will call for a correspondingly richer and fuller flavoured wine to match it.

Chicken and Turkey

Here there is an open choice between white and red, both being compatible. A cream sauce, though, would naturally indicate a white wine whereas plain roast turkey would be a good match for a light to medium flavoured red wine.

Game and Red Meat

Without a doubt, this is the domain of the red wines, be they from Burgundy, Bordeaux, Italy or California. The protagonists of all the regions can make their claim but it is really a question of personal choice.

Dessert

Here we enter the land of a group of wines that have regrettably lost much of their former popularity; the luscious, sweet wines of Sauternes and Barsac and the special selection of sweet wines from Germany. For most people these are too sweet for steady drinking, but a glass with a rich dessert can be delicious and even served alone with a ripe peach or other fruit, they can be a memorable experience.

After Dinner Wines

At this point we return to the fortified wines, notably port; ruby, tawny or noblest of all, vintage port. The wines of Madeira have a claim here, in particular, the luscious Malmsey, in a vat of which the unfortunate, or perhaps fortunate, Duke of Clarence met his death. Champagne could also again reappear, as a not-too-heavy late night drink. Its propagandists can also find a place for it throughout the meal and especially in its demi-sec version as a dessert wine.

Another point to bear in mind in selecting wines is that the cooking and the wines of different regions have grown up well together and therefore, when serving an Italian dish, it is often the most successful choice to serve an Italian wine and, for example, to serve a claret rather than a burgundy with an Entrecôte Bordelaise.

For the person who really wishes to learn about wine, the greatest discipline is that of making written notes on each wine tasted. For some reason, the mere committing to paper of an opinion organizes the mind wonderfully and forces greater definition than a mental note. The final discipline for the more experienced wine drinker is that of occasional blind tastings with friends when several wines, perhaps of very different price ranges, from the same or different regions are served without identification and then in a completely unprejudiced fashion the decision is made as to which is the best.

The enjoyment of wine is greatest when shared with friends who also enjoy it and I would like to thank those wine loving friends of mine, both professional and amateur, who over the years have given me so much by sharing with me their experience and expertise as well as their cellars.

9

Vineyards round the world

Left
A magnificent old Grenache. This is one of the thirteen varieties of vine that are needed to produce Châteauneuf du Pape. Most wines are made from one to three different varieties. The Grenache contributes mellowness of flavour as well as alcoholic content to the wine. This particular vine is at least fifty years old and is planted in the stony soil that is so typical of this region. The stones reflect the sun during the day and give off the heat they have absorbed at night, thus insuring full ripening of the grapes and consequent high alcoholic content.

Above
The Pinot Chardonnay is one of the great vines for white wines, producing a rather small yield but wines of great delicacy and style. It is the sole vine used for the great white Burgundies and is also planted in the Champagne Region. Like the Pinot Noir it is much prized in California as a varietal. Though its yield is comparatively small, the wine produced is of great quality. Another varietal which is unique to California is the Zinfandel which produces a lighter red wine that has some of the character of a Cabernet Sauvignon.

Left
The Chenin Blanc vine shown here is famous as the vine which produces the delicious Vouvray wine from near Tours in the Loire Valley. Vouvray is a soft, fruity white wine usually with a touch of sweetness, though a drier version is also made. This vine has also been very successful in producing a varietal wine in California. It is sometimes known as Pineau de la Loire. Other white wines of the Loire Valley, that are not made from the Chenin Blanc grape, include Muscadet, a very dry white wine, which comes from the region around Nantes and is popular in France with oysters. Two other fine dry white wines are from the districts of Pouilly Fumé and Sancerre.

Right
This Merlot vine in the vineyard at Château Terrefort, an excellent lesser growth in Bordeaux, plays a most important role in producing red Bordeaux wines. It produces a soft mellow wine and balances the more tannic astringency of the Cabernet Sauvignon, which gives character and elegance to the wine. Malbec and Petit Verdot, the other two vines that make up the typical Bordeaux vineyard give the vital ageing qualities and colour. It is the combination and balance between these four vines in the different vineyards that gives Bordeaux wines their great complexity of character.

Below
This new vineyard is being developed in the Soave Region near Verona in Northern Italy. The vines are trained along wires and the principle grape variety is the Trebbiano. The wine is light and delicate in flavour, a pale straw in colour and has a pleasant bouquet. It is probably the best known and most popular of Italy's white wines and goes well with the seafood and veal dishes of the country. Prior to planting a new vineyard, the land must be deep ploughed and should have been allowed to lie fallow for at least four years if it was previously used as a vineyard. The type of vines to be planted will be selected according to an analysis of the soil and the traditions and laws of the region. It is the effect of different soil conditions that causes the great variety of flavour in, for example, the white wines of the Côte d'Or region of Burgundy, all of which are made from the Pinot Chardonnay grape.

Top
The work of pruning is a very skilled and
important one and determines the future
production of the vine, both with regard
to quantity and quality. Here at Quinta
do Avaleda in the Minho Region of
Portugal, workers prune the high growing
vines that are trained on pergolas. It is
this method that is used to produce the
Vinho Verde, the refreshingly crisp white
wine of the region that generally has a
slight natural sparkle.

Above
This scene in the Jura Region on the
French-Swiss border shows both old and
new methods side by side. In the left of
the picture, the workers are hoeing the
ground by hand; but the vineyard is
planted in the modern fashion with the
rows of vines far enough apart to permit
a tractor to pass between them for

ploughing and to permit complete
mechanical cultivation of the vineyard.
Another type of tractor popular in the
Bordeaux and Burgundy regions is one
which has a high center that straddles the
vines and can be used for ploughing as
well as spraying, by means of a boom
attachment that will cover up to two
rows either side of the tractor. Jura
wines, the best known of which come
from around the town of Arbois, include
a great variety of white and rather deep
coloured rosé wines. The region produces
two very unusual wines: the Vin Jaune,
and the Vin de Paille. The best example
of Vin Jaune is Château Chalon, a
wine which is allowed to remain in
barrel from six to ten years before
bottling. During this period, a film of flor
similar to that found in the sherry forms
on the wine. The end result is a fairly dry
white wine with a most distinctive

flavour. The second type, the Vin de
Paille, is made from grapes which have
been allowed to dry out prior to crushing,
either by being laid out on beds of straw
or by hanging in storage rooms. This
produces a very rich, sweet wine which
lives for a long time in the bottle.

Right
Here in the Minho region is one of the
specially equipped tractors used for
spraying the vines against disease. This is
necessary in all vineyards and, according
to the weather during the year, will be
done from five to ten times. Should there
be a lot of rainfall, followed by warm
weather, the number of sprayings
against the danger of mildew will be
increased. The spray used is one made up
of copper sulphate, chalk and water.
Other specific sprays are used against
other pests as they appear.

Left

This view of Château Lafite shows a selection of Cabernet Sauvignon vines in the foreground. It can be seen how the earth is piled up around the roots of the vines, this both protects them from the frost in winter and also provides good drainage during the rest of the year. Notice how well this vineyard is tended with no weeds showing as befits a first growth. The vineyards of Château Lafite adjoin those of their rival, Château Mouton-Rothschild, so that they both have similar soil and weather conditions; however the ratio of the variety of vines planted is different. Lafite has a higher proportion of Merlot and Mouton has a higher proportion of Cabernet Sauvignon. It is perhaps this that gives Lafite that elegant softness in its great vintages. The outstanding vintages since the war have been 1945, 1949, 1953, 1959, 1961 and 1966 and 1970 which are as yet still too young to drink.

Below

The New York State vineyards in the Eastern United States are largely planted with vines of the species vitis labrusca, a hardy species that will survive extreme cold better than the vitis vinifera of Europe. Snows such as these are common during the winter at the Taylor Wine Company's vineyards in the Fingerlakes Region of New York State. In recent years, there has been considerable experiment with planting hybrid vines that combine the hardiness of the vitis labrusca with the more delicate flavour produced by the European vines.

Bottom

The Clos de Vougeot, one of the most famous vineyards in Europe, was founded by the Cistercian Monks in the twelfth century and remained the property of the Church until the French Revolution. The 124 acre vineyard is called a Clos because it is entirely enclosed by a stone wall. Today the vineyard is divided between approximately fifty different owners each of whom makes a slightly different wine. The best quality is considered to come from the top part of the vineyard away from the main road. There is also a small quantity of white wine made adjacent to the main vineyard which is sold as Clos Blanc de Vougeot. So important was the vineyard that it was a tradition for regiments of the French Army to present arms when passing the vineyard along the main road.

Left
This view, taken in the Fall as the leaves begin to turn, shows the great Corton vineyards with the wood of Corton at the top of the hill and the famous Corton Charlemagne vineyard directly below it. It will be noted that the best vineyards are on the higher slopes of the hill where they have the best drainage and the best exposure to the sunshine. This vineyard produces one of the greatest of all white Burgundies, considered by many to equal the great Montrachet. The wine is extremely elegant and has a fine, slightly nutty flavour which develops well in bottle. It has about the same weight as a Montrachet but is lighter than a Bâtard Montrachet.

Centre
The Château de Corton-Andre, with its beautiful decorated tile roof, dominates the village of Aloxe Corton from the main highway. It is the property of La Reine Pedauque, one of the largest vineyard owners and shippers of the region. The region is famous for its great white wine, Corton-Charlemagne, but most of the production is full bodied red wines. These are often a little hard when they are young but mature well and have a good flavour and character. The best known vineyards of the Château are the great first growths of Clos du Roi, Renardes and Pougets.

Below
This old Cabernet Sauvignon vine from near Yountville in California's Napa Valley is about 50 years old; unusually old for California. Such old vines, however, though their yield decreases each year, can contribute enormous character and quality to a wine and every vineyard owner who seeks quality always tries to retain a percentage of old vines in his vineyard.

Right
Here the town of Fleurie with its magnificent old church is pictured surrounded by its vineyards. The chief grape vine planted here is the Gamay which is used for all red Beaujolais. Fleurie is one of the finest crus of the Beaujolais region producing a typically light and deliciously fruity wine. It is also one that is very typically Beaujolais, compared to the richer, fuller wines of Moulin à Vent or Morgon. The Beaujolais vineyards are planted in the small, rolling foothills that lead up to the higher mountains in the background.

Left
This scene shows the vineyards of Hermitage in winter high above the Rhône Valley. The vines with the earth piled up around them for the winter have been severely pruned back and are in a dormant stage waiting for the sap to rise in the spring. The wines of Hermitage are very deep in colour, full bodied and long lasting with excellent flavour. The vine used is the Syrah. A quantity of a rather lighter wine called Crozes-Hermitage is also produced; it is similar in character to Hermitage but not equal to it in quality. In addition, a fine full bodied, dry white wine is made here.

Below
Vineyards on the slopes of Troodos Mountains in Cyprus. Cyprus wines, up until recently, have generally been of the sweet sherry and port kind so popular in England where they are sold at a rather low price. However, since the appearance of a report prepared by the late Fred Rossi in the 1950's the Cyprus Government has sponsored a programme to improve the quality and variety of the country's wines. In consequence these vineyards are beginning to produce some good quality table wines, as well as continuing with the traditional dessert types, the most famous of which was Commandaria recalling the time when Cyprus was the headquarters of the Knights of St John during the Crusades.

Top right
A beautiful scene showing the sun setting over the new Pinnacles Vineyards of Paul Masson close to the Pinnacles National Monument. These vineyards lie south of San Francisco on the slopes of a long valley running southeast from near Monterey, protected from the ocean by the Santa Lucia Mountains. The vines are planted far apart and are specially pruned to permit mechanical harvesting. Though the vineyards have only been planted recently, the first production indicates that their quality will be equal to if not superior to that of California's famed Napa Valley vineyards. This area has been planted exclusively with top varietal vines such as Cabernet Sauvignon, Pinot Chardonnay and Chenin Blanc.

Right
These vineyards are in the Barossa Valley district of South Australia. Vines have always been successful in the area and now irrigation by the Murray river has considerably increased production. Some of the best known wines are those of the Barossa Valley, which are planted with top quality varieties of vines. The whites are quite delicate in flavour and the reds are of good body and flavour. Wineries producing in this area include Penfold, Seppelt and Gramp.

Above

The heart of the Classico Chianti region of Tuscany is dominated by the magnificent old castle of Brolio on the hill in the background. Brolio has been the home of the Barons Ricasoli for a thousand years and the strength of its fortifications protected and preserved the family throughout the wars between Florence and Siena in the Middle Ages. It was the present Baron's grandfather who was responsible for setting up the original classification and blend for Chianti Classico, the inner region of the district, and for the adoption of the black cockerel seal which appears on every genuine bottle of Chianti Classico. The vineyard workers taking lunch in the foreground are well supplied with Brolio Chianti as it is the habit in all vineyards to issue a daily ration to each man in accordance with the size of his family.

Left

This vineyard in Argentina is a little similar to some in the Rioja District of Spain. However, in the center of the best vineyard region at Mendoza the vineyards appear much greener, as they are irrigated by the melting snows and glaciers of the

22

Andes Mountains, whose foothills commence at the Western limit of the vineyards. Here a wide variety of top quality varietals such as Cabernet, Merlot and Malbec are grown. There is also a certain amount of Chardonnay and Riesling planted for the white wines.

Right

Typical, steeply sloping vineyards tower above the banks of the beautiful Moselle river. Probably the most famous vineyard in Germany is at Bernkastel situated in the Middle Moselle and is known as the Doctor. The wine of Bernkasteler Doctor is the epitome of fine Moselle. It is delicate in flavour with a touch of fruit and also sweetness yet with an elegance and delicacy of aroma all its own. Two other fine vineyards whose product is sometimes blended with that of the Doctor are Graben and Badstube. The soil is mainly a shaly slate and one of the additional labours of the Moselle vignerons, especially after heavy rains, is to gather the soil that has slid to the bottom of the hill and haul it up to its former position at the top of the vineyard.

The vintage, production & bottling of wine

Below left
Picking at Bacharach on the Middle Rhine. This area was an important one in the eighteenth century because of its strategic position as a port on the Rhine. Little wine is exported under the name of the village, though there is one well known vineyard, Schloss Furstenburg.

Below centre
This vintage scene is in the heart of the Beaujolais country at Moulin à Vent. Here the pickers are bringing their small pails of the Gamay grapes, which produce the greatest Beaujolais wine, to the man who will carry these to the large tubs for transport to the winery. In the background, we see the windmill, today minus its vanes, that gives its name to the area. The windmill is situated on top of a small hill and can be seen for miles around. The area that produces the wines of Moulin à Vent is partly within the commune of Chenas and partly in that of Romaneche-Thorins. This wine is considered to be the heaviest of all Beaujolais.

Below right
In this picturesque scene on the Island of Crete, the grapes are trained on pergolas and the large bunches are here being harvested by local women. This method of training was popular in Italy and the Mediterranean areas in ancient times and many homes would have a terrace shaded by a pergola of grapes so that the family could sit outside in the evening and reach up and pick the grapes directly from the vine. Crete, like most of the Mediterranean area, produces wine that is almost all consumed locally and rarely exported.

Top right
Here the men, having collected the grapes picked by the individual pickers, tip them into a large tub mounted on a cart which will then take the grapes to the cellars where the wine will actually be made. This vintage scene is from Wachau in Austria. It is an excellent producing area along the Danube, chiefly famous, like most of Austria for its white wines. Only about 15 per cent of the wine produced is red. The best known wines are those from Krems and also Gumpoldskirchner from south of Vienna. The popular grape varieties include the Riesling, Grunerveltliner, Muller-Thurgau and Furmint.

Opposite left
The vineyards of South Africa are divided into two main groups: the first consists of the vineyards of the Coastal and Cape Province areas, and includes such well known districts as Paarl and Stellenbosch which produce the finer table wines and ports and sherries. The second group of vineyards are in the Little Karoo area which produces the sweeter dessert wines and wines for distilling into Brandy. This photograph shows the vintage in progress at Worcester, which lies on the border between the Cape and Little Karoo districts. The grapes here are large in size and in general the yields of the Little Karoo district are much higher than those of the Cape.

Opposite right
In parts of the Beaujolais region, a slightly different system of collecting the grapes prevails. The pickers fill smaller tubs with protruding handles and carry them at intervals to the end of the rows. The men collect the tubs, carrying them slung from a pole. When the trailer is fully loaded, it will be towed by tractor to the press house.

Above
Over the last few years the development of the mechanical harvester has progressed considerably. Originally there were two types: those that removed the grapes by suction and those that removed them by beating the vines so that the grapes fell into the collecting sections beneath. However, the suction type tended to absorb leaves, twigs and insects and now it seems that the beating type of machine will be the one of the future. Experiments continue however as to the best method of training the vines in order that they may be harvested with least damage to the vine. Here a mechanical harvester is seen in operation at the Taylor Wine

Company vineyards in New York State. The accompanying truck collects the grapes and takes them to the winery to complete crushing and fermentation.

Right
In contrast to the mechanical harvester this small, family operation at Oppenheim in the Rheinhessen district of Germany includes pressing on the spot. The freshly gathered grapes from the vineyards are tipped directly into a small crushing machine which will break their skins as they drop into the tub below. This tub will then be taken to the family cellar for fermenting. This type of operation is limited to the small family vineyards

which are very common in the Rheinhessen region. For larger scale operations, including the cooperative groups of wine growers, the grapes are taken to the central press houses, where they are then destalked and crushed and fermented in large lots. Increasing numbers of the wine growers in this region beiong to cooperatives and do not make the wine themselves but concentrate on producing grapes. The district of Oppenheim is one of the best in the region and its most famous vineyards are those of Goldberg, Herrenberg, Krotenbrunnen and Sacktrager. However, many of these names will disappear under the new German wine law.

Left

These white wine grapes are being loaded into a modern cylindrical-type press at a winery in Germany. Presses like these are very popular for white wines all over the world and are generally of two types. In one, a rubber tube in the center of the press is gradually inflated forcing the juice out of the grapes, through the wooden slats of the press and into fermenting vats. In the second type, the two ends of the press gradually move towards the center and rotating chains keep the mass of grapes broken up during this pressing period. The best wine comes from the earliest pressing before the pressure becomes too severe.

Left

The well equipped 'cuvier' or vat house at Château La Mission Haut Brion in the Graves district, showing the vat in which fermentation takes place. This type of vat, which is generally glass lined, is replacing wooden vats for fermentation due to greater ease of maintenance and, in particular, due to the fact that they are much easier to keep clean and sterile in between each batch. Once the fermentation is finished, the wine will be run off into 50 gallon oak barrels for aging.

Below

A picture taken in the Canadian winery, Château Gai, shows a vat of red wine in full fermentation. The 'cap' of grape skins floats to the top of the vat and forms a layer through which the gas forces itself creating the pink froth that is seen here. This violent fermentation will last for about three days and becomes progressively less forceful. Once the fermentation is over, the wine is run off from this vat for aging in larger vats or small oak barrels.

Right

A magnificent old wooden press at Clos des Langres, a walled vineyard that forms the boundary between the Côte de Nuits and the Côte de Beaune. A few of these old presses remain and though this one is still in working order, it is not used regularly. Another fine old medieval press can be found at the Clos de Vougeot. In this type of press, the grapes were often packed between seperators woven from osiers and the juice flowed off from a spout in the center at the front of the press. A hand operated winch would be used to haul in the rope that turned the screw of the press.

Top left
The craft of the cooper or barrel maker
is one of the oldest in the world and
anyone wishing to enter this old craft
must first undergo a long apprenticeship.
Though modern aids have been
introduced, much of the work must still
be done by skilled hands and here in a
London cooperage we see the cooper at
work making staves for a small tub or
barrel. Once the staves are shaped and
curved, the exact number must be set
within iron hoops and heated over a fire
inside the half formed barrel before the
headpieces are inserted at either end and
the hoops are tightened.

Left
This subterranean cellar with its vaulted
stone roof is very typical of the Burgundy
region. The cellar, which is often damp
with mould growing on the walls is
maintained at a constant cold temperature
of around 55°F and it is here that the
wines are aged in barrel following the
first fermentation in the vat. Red wines
will generally rest up to two years before
bottling and the white wines about
18 months, though nowadays the lighter,
less expensive white wines often spend
most of their aging time in large glass
lined vats to keep them fresher and
fruitier to suit today's taste.

Above
Magnificent old storage vats in the
cellars of the Château de Riquewihr,
the property of the noted Alsatian wine
shipper, Dopff and Irion. Riquewihr,
whose vineyards are considered to be the
best in Alsace, is one of the last remaining
walled towns in Europe and is most
picturesque with its old stone houses
with their overhanging second floors and
the many flower-filled window boxes.
The vineyards of Alsace (the French
Rhineland) are very well situated as they
are protected by the Vosges Mountains
from the west and are exposed to the sun
and heat of the Rhine Valley. They tend
to produce fuller flavoured wines than
those of the German Rhine land.

Right
Here at one of Paul Masson's
California wineries wines are shown
aging in small, 50 gallon oak barrels.
The younger wines in the foreground
have loose stoppers in order to
permit any excess gas to escape
following fermentation and to allow easy
refilling of the casks. Older wines are
stored on the tall rack system in the
background. It is generally agreed that
aging in small oak barrels can contribute
substantially to the quality of the wine,
especially to that of red wine.

Above
A scene in a Burgundian cellar showing the old method of bottling by hand which has now been almost entirely replaced by mechanical methods except in the very smallest cellars. First the cellar master ensures that the wine has become completely bright and clear. He then taps the cask by boring a hole and inserting a spigot immediately above the level of the sediment. The bottles are filled by hand ensuring a continuous flow of wine so as not to stir up the sediment by stopping the flow. The bottles would then be corked by hand and laid away for aging in bottle.

Above right
This Burgundian cellar master is making one of his regular checks of the progress of the aging wine in barrels. He uses the pipette or wine thief to draw the wine from the barrel and taste it in his silver tastevin or tasting cup. This shallow, dimpled silver vessel reflects the colour of the wine so that he can check the clarity and he will then nose it to check the aroma and finally taste it. During the period of aging, the wines are tasted frequently and checked in order to determine the correct time at which to rack the wines into fresh barrels.

Right
At Château d'Yquem, the only vineyard of the Sauternes district to be classified as a First growth, the cellarmaster is checking samples of the new vintage early the following year. The barrels still have only loose glass stoppers in them to allow the fermentation to continue and any gas to escape. The wine is still not clear in the glass due to the continuing fermentation. This means that the yeast still present in the wine creates the consequent cloudiness. Here, as is normal in the Bordeaux district, many of the cellars are at ground level and space is less at a premium than in the Burgundy region where the barrels are normally stacked two tiers high.

Above
Another large scale industry in
Argentina, the third largest wine-
producing country in the world.
This vat at Bodegas Penaflor is probably
the largest interior vat in the world with
a capacity of 5,000,000 litres. About 30'
high with its interior pillars, it has the
appearance of a ball room and to
inaugurate the vat, a dinner was held
for 1,000 people inside it complete with
an orchestra.

Right
The modern bottling line at Mateus Rosé,
where stainless steel conditioning tanks
are used and the whole area is kept
scrupulously clean to prevent any
contamination of the wine during
bottling. The bottles are loaded on to
the conveyor belt at one end of the
bottling line where they are sterilized
and then placed in the rotating filling
machine and on down the conveyor belt
to the corking machine. After bottling,
young wines generally proceed for
immediate labelling and packing into

cases but wines that require further aging
will generally not be labelled at this
point but sent to cellars for storage until
required. In the case of Mateus Rosé, the
wine is packed immediately into cases
ready for shipment. At many cellars in
Europe, the cool damp conditions would
in any case cause the labels to deteriorate
and also when wines are for shipment
abroad it would not be possible to label
until the final destination of the wines
is known since the legal requirements
for labelling vary from country to
country.

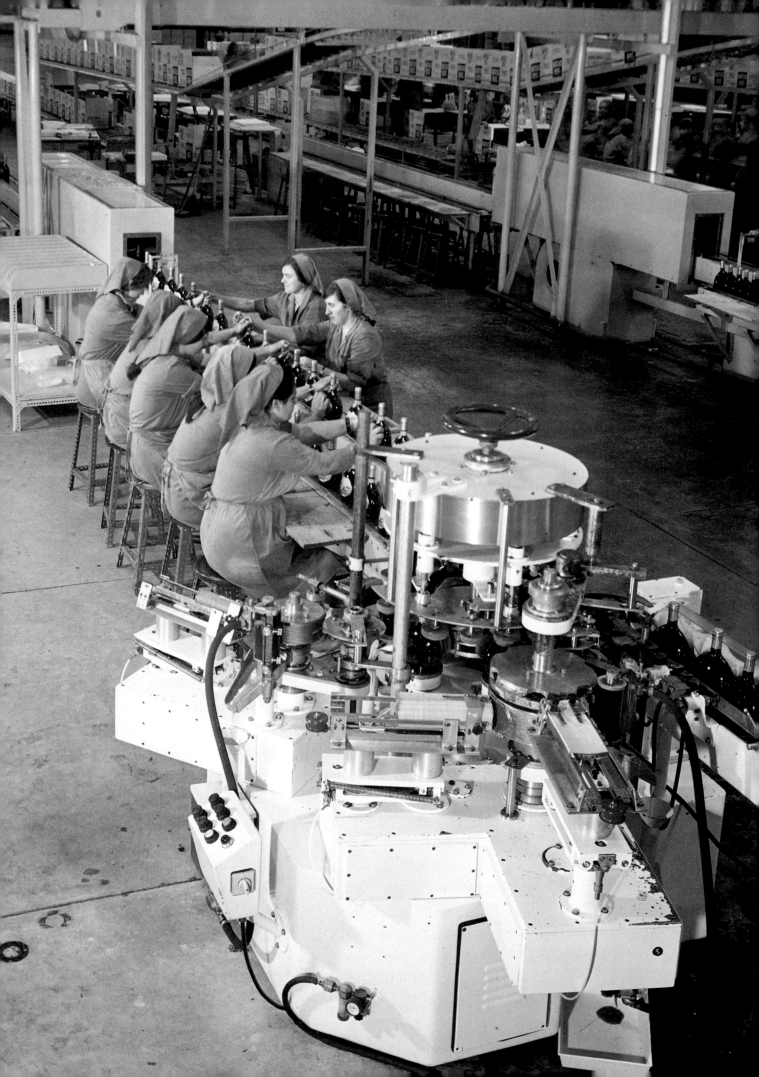

Table wines & the great first growths

Below

It is the tower in the vineyard that gives the name to Château Latour. The actual Château can be seen in the background. This vineyard was classified together with Château Lafite, Château Margaux and Château Haut Brion as the four First growths of the Medoc in the famous classifications made in 1855 on the occasion of the Paris Exposition. Château Mouton-Rothschild, which at the time was classified at the head of the Second growths, is indisputably regarded today as worthy of First growth rank and generally fetches a higher price than most of the other first growths. Château Latour has the enviable reputation of producing better wine than any of its peers in the less successful vintages, in addition to the superb wine that it produces in the great vintages.

Right

Here are three First growths of the Medoc, according to the 1855 classification. The fourth wine was Château Haut Brion from the Graves district. Château Lafite, classed as number one, produces outstanding wine in the great vintages but it is considered by many that Château Latour and Mouton-Rothschild perhaps do better in the lesser vintages. The 1952 Latour shown here was overshadowed by the great 1953 vintage; it matured more slowly but finally produced an excellent wine. The classical columns of Château Margaux are shown on the label, and it is indeed one of the most beautiful châteaux of the Medoc. In addition to its fine red wine, a small amount of dry white wine is made under the name of Pavillon Blanc de Château Margaux.

Above
Château Lascombes, a Second growth from the Margaux district, was until recently the property of Mr Alexis Lichine, the noted wine expert and author, but was recently sold by him to the big English brewery group, Bass Charrington. Flag poles around the Château carry the flags of the many countries to which its wine is sold and they hold an interesting art exhibition each summer of paintings connected with wine. The cellar is also one of the prettiest in the Medoc.

Top right
The beautiful rose pink Château of Loudenne lies at St Yzans in the extreme north of the Medoc. Because of the particular site of the vineyard it produces a finer wine than its neighbours. In addition to its agreeable red wine, a small amount of excellent, light, dry wine is produced. Loudenne shares with Château Margaux the distinction of being one of the few Châteaux to produce a white wine in the Medoc.

The Château was bought in the middle of the eighteenth century by the famous English wine and spirit family of Gilbey, a truly pioneering Victorian family who set up outposts not only in France but also in Canada, Australia and South Africa. The Château is now owned by Gilbey, S.A., a part of the International Distillers and Vintners Combine.

Below
Château Pichon Longueville in Pauillac is also a Second growth. This vineyard is adjacent to that of Château Latour. The château, identified as that of the Comtesse de Lalande, lies on the river side of the 'Route Du Vin', the road that runs through the heart of the Medoc. There is however another Pichon Longueville vineyard known as Baron which with its Château was built immediately opposite on the other side of the road. Pichon Longueville Baron produces about 6,000 cases of wine each year whereas the Pichon Longueville Comtesse makes about 12,000, both large productions for this area.

Previous pages
A beautiful stretch of the Rhine near
Bacharach showing the vineyards rising
steeply from the river on either side. The
vineyards are well exposed to the sun and
also benefit from the reflection of its rays
by the river. The wines of the Rhine
range from the fairly dry wines in this
northern section to the fuller flavoured
wines of the Rhinegau and to the full
rich and, in many cases, sweet wines
of the Palatinate further south.

Above
These grapes of the Riesling variety have
been affected by the bacteria known as
Botrytis. This mould attacks the
overripe grapes and is known as the
'noble rot'. It is responsible for the
luscious white wines of the Sauternes
district of Bordeaux as well as the
fabulous Trockenbeerenauslese of
Germany. The mould penetrates the
skin of the grapes and gradually draws off
the excess liquid. As a result, when the
grapes are pressed, the remaining juice is
of extremely high concentration of sugar
and glycerine while still having a
necessary balance of acidity. This
produces a wine of tremendous
concentration and flavour and quite
remarkable bouquet. However, it only
occurs in certain weather conditions
and there is no guarantee that in any
one vintage it will appear.

Below
Schloss Johannisberg is one of the great
wine estates of Germany. The estate is
the property of the Metternich family to
whom it was given as a reward for their
excellent service to the Hapsburgs. In the
magnificent vineyards that overlook the
Rhine, they make the several different
types of wine that are specified in such
detail on German labels. For example the
Spatlese or late gathered wines, the
Auslese, in which a special selection is
made of the ripest bunches, and the
Trockenbeerenauslese, produced from a
special selection of individual overripe
berries which have been attacked by a
particular fungus that draws off all the
surplus moisture. This last is a fantastic,
rich nectar that is a true experience to
taste. However, at Schloss Johannisberg
these wines are identified by the colour
of the capsule which varies for each one.

Right
The terraced vineyards in the middle
Rhine region gives some indication of how
difficult many of the Rhine and Moselle
vineyards are to cultivate. Apart from
the cost of hand labour, which is a
problem for many forms of agriculture,
it is becoming increasingly difficult to
get young people to go to work on the
land when there are easier and better
paid jobs available.

Above

Some of the finest vineyards of the Riquewihr Region of Alsace. The wines of Alsace, all of which are fairly dry, are named after the grape variety from which they are produced. The best are the Riesling and Gewurztraminer, a very spicy full flavoured wine which is very distinctive of Alsace.

Right

This assortment of wine bottles is shown in a London wine merchant's ancient cellars. The different shapes indicate the various regions and types of wines and compile a good selection of what might be expected from a representative wine store or private cellar. In the extreme foreground, lying on its side, is a black bottle of the type used for vintage Port and also vintage Madeiras. Behind it is a traditional red Burgundy bottle and the easily recognizable label of Château D'Yquem, the great Sauternes. Lying down to the left is a bottle of the great Château Mouton-Rothschild, easily recognizable by the distinctive band at the top of the label that changes with each vintage and is designed by a different artist each year. Beyond that is a White Burgundy bottle, sitting above is the distinctive bottle of the White Italian Soave of Bolla. In the top right hand corner of the picture, are bottles of Dry Sherry, the delightful aperitif, and next to them, in the middle of the top case, a fine German Rhine wine, Schloss Vollrads, which leans against a delicate dry, white wine from the Loire, Sancerre. A collection such as this indeed spans a wide portion of the spectrum of wines.

left

These bottles represent two great wines that should be included amongst the top flight of Bordeaux. The motto of Château Mouton-Rothschild 'Premier ne Puis, Second ne Daigne, Mouton Suis', sums up its position succinctly, while Château Cheval Blanc is one of the two great growths of St Emilion. The immediate post war vintages were of superb quality due to the fine weather conditions and also due to the fact that since the beginning of the war in 1939, practically no vineyards had been replanted and so the average age of the vines was higher than usual. 1945, 1947, 1948 and 1949 were excellent years; 1950 was good, but not quite in the same class. The 1945, in particular, was extremely tannic when young and took some twenty years, in many cases, to reach maturity.

Bottom left

The initiation ceremonies of the Chevaliers de Tastevin in progress during one of their banquets at the Clos de Vougeot. The robed members of the Grand Council first hear a brief introduction hailing the qualities of the new candidate who is then dubbed on the shoulder with an old vine root, kissed on both cheeks and presented with his ribbon and silver tastevin, the Burgundian wine tasting cup. After the installation ceremonies, a banquet for several hundred people is held in the great hall of the Clos de Vougeot. During the dinner, the Cadets de Bourgogne entertain the company with local Burgundian wine songs and frequent 'Bans Bourguignons', the chorus of the society.

Right

A rich setting in which to eat and drink, the Café Royal, London has an excellent cellar. This 1937 Clos Vougeot might seem at first sight to be too old. However it is undoubtedly still an excellent bottle, as the label shows that it came from the remarkable collection of Doctor Barolet. This private cellar, consisting of large quantities of top quality Burgundies of very old vintages, was recently discovered following the Doctor's death in the Burgundian region. The wines were later sold at auction and have turned out to be of excellent quality despite their age, as they had remained undisturbed until their recent shipment. The important point with old wines is that unless their history is known, they are not often good buys.

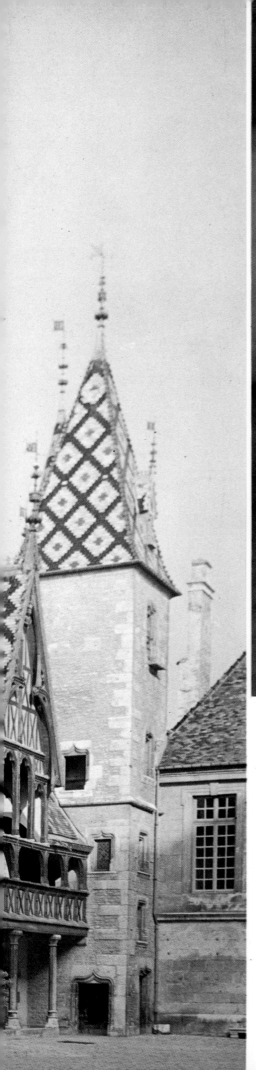

Above
Château Ausone is the second great wine of St Emilion, and a bottle of the great 1953 vintage, is shown here. The wine of this year had a very attractive, mellow quality and matured fairly quickly. The great Château d'Yquem tops the list of wines from the Sauternes district, and stands in a class of its own quite apart from its nearest competitors. Château d'Yquem is one of the few white wines that needs age in bottle to develop its full flavour and which is also a long lasting wine. The 1959 vintage was particularly good for Yquem.

Left
Hospices de Beaune, or the old people's hospital in the town of Beaune, must be one of the most photographed buildings in the world. It is a beautiful old building and its decorated tile roof is truly a masterpiece. The hospital was founded in 1443 by Nicolas Rollin, who was the Chancellor of the Dukes of Burgundy. Endowed by Rollin and other later benefactors with vineyards in the region, its income comes from the sale of the wine produced at those vineyards. There is an annual auction sale on the third Sunday in November which is one of the major events of the wine world as it is the first indication of the prices to be fetched by the wines of the new vintage. The different lots or Cuvees are sold under the name of the original donor and carry the special label of the Hospices de Beaune. The auction is part of the 'Trois Glorieuses', or three glorious days when there is also a dinner of the Chevaliers de Tastevin at Clos de Vougeot and the wine grower's lunch or 'Paulee de Meursault'.

Below
Château Langoa Barton is a most attractive Château of classic lines and is the property of Mr Ronald Barton, whose ancestors in the eighteenth century founded the great Bordeaux shipping house of Barton and Guestier. In the cellars of Château Langoa Barton, they not only produce and age their own Third growth but also a portion of the Leoville vineyard, a Second growth known as Leoville Barton. These two great Saint Julians both have a distinctive individual character of their own. The Barton is the finer and more complex wine of the two, and is particularly noted for its aging qualities.

Left
Some of the noblest wines of Burgundy are represented here. Montrachet, should, according to Dumas, be 'drunk on one's knees with head bared', and is the acknowledged king of the white wines of Burgundy. It also, like Château d'Yquem, has a long life in bottle. The great Richebourg from the village of Vosne Romanee, which encompasses so many of the great Red Burgundies, is a superbly soft, velvety, yet complex flavoured wine that requires many years to reach its peak. The world has to be satisfied with an annual production of less than two-and-a-half thousand cases. Chambertin is another of the giants of Burgundy and is said to have been the favourite wine of the Emperor Napoleon. This bottle is of the magnificent 1945 vintage. Again there is a very small production of only just over three thousand cases.

Above
Picking at Château Tahbilk, one of the best known Australian vineyards which is situated near Seymour to the northeast of Melbourne, in the state of Victoria. Victoria vineyards suffered in the early years from phylloxeria and though the wines are of excellent quality, the area of vineyards was much reduced. The State is also noted for the production of Sparkling wines in the Great Western area northwest of Melbourne. As in California, most Australian wines are sold under the name of the producer and type with some wineries producing individual branded types. There is also considerable production of Port and Sherry styles, for which there used to be a big market in the United Kingdom.

Right
The rugged vineyard country of the Rioja district in northern Spain, about half way between Madrid and the French border. This is generally acknowledged to be the finest district for Spanish table wines, with the red wines of Valdepenas, south of Madrid, coming close. It produces dry white wines,

but its real pride are its magnificent full bodied red wines which age extremely well both in barrel and in bottle. There is a tendency in Spain to keep wine longer in casks than would be normal elsewhere. The wines here are sold under the brands of the different wineries that produce them, the most famous being Marques de Riscal.

Below
This attractive vineyard scene is in the Fingerlakes region of New York State. The lakes themselves are very important to the production of wine as they temper the severe climate of this region and help reflect the limited sunshine onto the vine. A wide variety of table wines are made as well as sparkling wines.

Left
A beautiful photograph of the hilltop town of Orvieto to the north of Rome. The town itself is most attractive and has a very famous church with a beautifully tiled exterior. The white wine that is produced here is also traditionally bottled in a raffia covered bottle, similar to the Chianti but a little squatter. The wine is all white and was traditionally rich and sweeter or 'Aboccato', but now a drier, clean tasting wine called Secco is made here. It tends to be rather high in alcohol for a white wine.

Below
This young woman in the Tuscany region is weaving the raffia container and base for the traditional Chianti bottle. It is becoming more and more difficult to get this work done and, as a result, the price of the traditional bottle is becoming much more expensive resulting in more and more Chianti being bottled in the traditional Bordeaux shaped bottle. Attempts to find an alternative design that will be as attractive as the traditional raffia covered bottles have so far been unsuccessful.

Previous pages
Vineyards in the region of Bardolino on
the shores of Lake Garda in Northern
Italy. The wine is light and clean in
flavour and goes well with much of the
northern Italian cuisine. Further west in
the direction of Venice are the vineyards
of Valpolicella and also the vineyards of
Soave, which produce what is probably
Italy's best known white wine; it is
fresh and delicate and should always
be drunk young. Most shippers of
this area (known as the Veneto) will
ship all three wines.

Above
Bernkasteler Doctor is the most famous
wine of the Moselle district and 1959 was
one of the greatest vintages in Germany.
Schloss Vollrads is one of the great
estates of the Rheingau and produces
many different grades. Nierstein is one of
the best districts of the Rheinhessen
district, which produces softer, mellower
wines than the Rheingau and the
Niersteiner Hipping Rehbach is one
of the best vineyards.

Champagne and sparkling wines

Here at the Abbey of Hautvillers, overlooking the Valley of the Marne, is found the memorial to Dom Perignon, the cellarer of the Abbey, who is credited not only with discovering that by blending the wines of the different parts of the Champagne region a finer wine could be produced, but also with the introduction of the cork to seal the bottles, which causes the sparkling quality of Champagne. Champagne was originally a still wine.

Above

In this scene we see the culmination of the complicated production process of French Champagne. To the right of the picture, the bottles are received neck down having passed through a freezing solution that freezes the sediment above the cork. The disgorger then removes the cork and the pellet of sediment in the special hooded machine. The bottle is then placed in a filling machine which replaces the missing wine and adds the amount of sweetness required. The circular machine holding the bottles can be clearly seen with the pipes running from the barrel above to the containers of Champagne and sweetening wine. The bottles finally pass to a corking machine, and are then shaken to ensure the proper mixing of the sweetening wine before being placed in cases.

Right

Mr Victor Lanson, principal of the Champagne house of that name, in the vineyards during the vintage with the famous windmill of Verzenay in the background. These vineyards form part of the Mountain of Rheims section which are largely planted in Pinot Noir. Most traditional Champagne cuvees use about 80 per cent Pinot Noir with the balance being Pinot Chardonnay. A traditional cuvee will last longer in bottle than a Blanc du Blanc made entirely from Pinot Chardonnay.

Following pages

These vineyards are in the neighbourhood of Epernay in the Champagne district of France. The Champagne district is divided into three sections: the Valley of the Marne, of which these vineyards form part; the Côte des Blancs, which runs south from the Valley of the Marne and which, as its name implies, is planted mainly with the white Pinot Chardonnay grapes; and the large area of the Mountain of Rheims. It is the art of blending the produce of grapes from all parts of the Champagne District which gives each individual brand its special character. The word 'cuvee' is used in the Champagne district to denote these blends.

Above
These are the *pupitres*, which form a vital part of the Champagne process, and which are situated in one of the old Roman chalk pits in the region of Rheims. It is in these racks that the Champagne bottles are placed for the *remuage*, or riddling process that works the sediment down to the neck of the bottle. The *remueur* has the delicate task of riddling the bottles every couple of days and gradually moving them from a horizontal to a vertical position in order to work all the sediment down onto the top of the cork for easy removal. This process can take up to three months and a skilled man can work as many as 20,000 bottles per day.

Top right
Schramsberg, near Calistoga, in the northern part of the Napa Valley,

is a Californian winery which produces Champagne exclusively and uses the classic Champagne method. On the left of these tunnels are the wines in pupitre, with the aging wine on the right. This winery, which was developed in the late nineteenth century is most interesting inasmuch as the cellars were tunnelled out of the rock by Chinese coolies brought up from San Francisco. Robert Louis Stevenson wrote of Schramsberg in his book, 'The Silverado Squatters', written during his stay in California. After being defunct for many years, the winery was resurected by Jack and Jamie Davies in 1966 where they concentrate on the production of the highest quality Champagne. This was the Champagne that President Nixon chose to serve during his famous journey to Peking.

Above
A typical Champagne cellar showing

bottles undergoing aging following the period of second fermentation in the bottle. It is this fermentation that produces the sparkle in Champagne. The cellars of the Champagne region hold literally millions of bottles of Champagne in their long, underground tunnels which have been carved out of the chalk over the years. The average Champagne cellar will contain one million bottles per mile of cellars.

Right
In Koblenz where the Moselle meets the Rhine are the sparkling wine cellars of Deinhard & Company, where they produce their Sekt, as German sparkling wines are called. Production takes place on a very large scale using wines from many regions to produce the final blend. The domestic consumption per capita in Germany is very high compared with that of other countries.

Fortified wines

Fortified wines are wines that are made naturally from grapes but, at some stage in their production, brandy is added to raise the strength from a normal 12 to 14 per cent to between 18 and 22 per cent. They are produced mainly in Spain, Portugal, the United States and Canada, South Africa, Australia and New Zealand, as well as the islands of Madeira and Sicily, the most famous types being Sherry, Port, Madeira and Marsala.

Right
These vineyards are at Puerto de Santa Maria near Cadiz in Southern Spain. The very white, chalky soil here is called algariza and produces the light, delicate, dry Sherry called Manzanilla. Manzanilla has a special tang which is said to be due to being grown and matured on the edge of the Atlantic ocean. Fino Sherry, also a very dry one, which is produced inland near Jerez de la Frontera in the same soil and from the same grapes does not have this special flavour.

Left
The Palomino grape vine that is shown here is the basic vine for all Sherries. There are a few other grapes such as Pedro Ximenez that are grown to produce sweetening wine for the Medium and Cream Sherries.

Below left
One of the unique processes in the production of sherry is the practice of leaving the grapes in the sun for a period to reduce the moisture in them and thus increase the sugar content. Here we see grapes that have been brought in from the vineyards in the background being unloaded from donkeys and placed on the typical round esparto grass mats. After this, the grapes are taken to the presses. Some are still pressed by being trodden in large square troughs called Lagares by men in specially nailed boots.

Right
After the violent first fermentation of the sherry it is put into large wooden barrels, called butts, and a small amount of brandy is added to the wine to bring the strength up to about 18 per cent, thus stabilizing the wine. (An additional amount of brandy is added at the end of the aging process, rather more in the sweeter Cream Sherries than in the light Dry Finos.) Finally there is a unique process called the Solera System. The wine is stored in a series of long rows of barrels and when sherry is required for shipment a small amount is drawn from each of the oldest line of barrels. These barrels, in turn, are then refilled from the next oldest row and so back through as much as four or five different rows. The last row is filled up with the wine of the recent vintage. In this way, continuity is maintained and it is said that the older wine educates the young wine.

Left
The vineyard country of the Douro valley lies about 100 miles inland from the town of Oporto which gives its name to Port. The country is wild and rugged and sparsely populated. The vineyards all have to be terraced which is laborious work and dynamite is often needed to prepare the rocky soil to receive new vines. Port is produced from a variety of different vines, including the Touriga Bastardo, Mourisco, and the Pintas.

Right
Harvest time is a happy time — not only to celebrate when the grapes have been picked but also to be enjoyed while the work goes on. These women in their regional dress are picking the port grapes from very large vines at Aveleda in Portugal, removing from each cluster any defective berry which could start the fermenting process, and laying them in the vintage baskets.

Left
The baskets, here covered with vine leaves to shield the grapes from the sun, are then carried by the men or hoisted onto donkeys or oxen and brought to the *lagar*, the great stone tank of the wine press. It is interesting to note one of the differences between the processing of port and sherry grapes. Here the port grapes are covered by vine leaves to keep them cool on their journey to the press, whereas the sherry grapes are laid out on the ground in the sun to dry off before being transported.

Above
The Douro region was one of the last places in the world where the treading of grapes by man continued and there are a very few spots today where it still can be seen. Treading of the grapes usually took place at night and the men used to sing and play to help them pass the long night hours. Fermentation then begins, and before the fermentation has finished and all the sugar has been converted into alcohol, brandy is added to stop the fermentation. This means that a certain amount of the rich sweetness still remains, and it is this that gives port its special character.

Left
For many years, the Barco Rabelo, a
shallow draught sailing vessel, was the
only way of bringing the wine down from
the Douro for blending and aging in the
shippers lodges, or cellars, at Vila Nova
de Gaia at the mouth of the Douro.
Today the railroad carries most of this
traffic. The journey down by river
required skillful boatmen as the river is
swift flowing and there were many rocks
and rapids to be negotiated on the way.

The youngest port is described as Ruby
on account of its colour and the shippers
will blend different lots together with
older vintages to maintain the consistent
quality of their brand of Ruby. Likewise,
as the Port grows older it becomes tawny
in colour and develops a nutty aroma
and mellow smooth flavour. The shippers
will maintain extensive stocks of old

tawny's for blending purposes and
several brands are put on the market
with an average age of as much as 20
years. The most renowned port of all
is vintage port, which, instead of being
allowed to mature in barrels like the
Ruby and Tawny, is bottled after two
years and ages in bottle. A good vintage
port will need at least 10 years in
bottle to develop and can last for
as much as 50 or more years.

Above
The Island of Madeira is situated in the
Atlantic, some 350 miles off the Moroccan
coast and is famous for its fortified wines.
The island was discovered by the
Portuguese navigator, Zarco, in 1418 and
legend has it that he set fire to the heavily
forested island which burned for seven
years. This, coupled with the volcanic

soil, has always made Madeira extremely
fertile and it is possible to grow an
enormous variety of fruits, vegetables,
sugar cane, in addition to magnificent
flowers, without much difficulty. The
island is extremely steep and, as can be
seen here, the vines are planted to best
advantage on the hillsides which run
steeply down from the center of the
island to the sea in the background. After
fermentation, brandy is added to the
wine, which is then stored for a period of
approximately six months in specially
heated rooms which raise the temperature
to something over 100°F and gently
lower it again. There is a great range of
different types from the delicate dry but
full flavoured Sercial to the luscious rich
Malmsey.

Acknowledgements

The publishers would like to thank the following organizations and individuals for their kind permission to reproduce the pictures in this book:

Alan Foley Photographic Library 21 bottom, 52   **Armando Diaz** 64 right   **Bass Charrington Vintners Ltd** 12 centre, 55   **E Bauer, Bavaria Verlag** 25 top   **Bavaria Verlag** 23   **F H C Birch, Sonia Halliday Photographs Ltd** 20 bottom, 24 right   **G Brinkman, Bavaria Verlag** 42 top   **Browne Vintners Co** 51   **Gerald Clyde, Michael Holford** 67   **F Corbineau, Réalités** 46 bottom   **Dopff & Irion, S.A. Riquewihr** 31 top   **Robert Estall** 42 bottom **Foods from France, Inc.** New York 14 bottom, 64 left, 64 bottom **Galitzine Chant Russell & Partners Ltd** 38, 45   **German Wine Information Bureau,** New York 28 top, 43   **Gilbey, S.A.** 39 top

Percy Hennell endpapers, 2-3, 6-7, 11, 12 left, 13, 14 top, 15, 18 centre, 19, 20 top, 25 right, 30 top, 35-6, 39 bottom, 48, 53, 54, 59-63, 65-6, 68-71   **Eckhart van Houten, George Rainbird Ltd** 22 top, 56-7   **Dr R Lorenz, Bavaria Verlag** 27   **Paul Masson Vineyards** 21 top, 31 bottom   **M Nahmias, Réalités** 17   **Ron Nielson** 28 bottom, 34   **Octopus Books Ltd** 1 (by courtesy of Hedges and Butler Ltd) 37, 46 top, 49, 50, 58 (by courtesy of the Café Royal, London) 47   **La Reine Pedauque** 9, 29   **Philippe Roualet** 10, 16 bottom, 18 top, 30 bottom, 32   **Howard Silvester, Rapho** 44   **Spectrum Colour Library** 40-1   **Stellenbosch** 25 left   **Taylor Wine Co, Inc** 16 top, 26, 52 bottom **Noel E Vargas** 22 bottom, 34   **Sabine Weiss, Rapho** 24 left, 24 centre, 33   **Dr James A White III** 18 bottom   **Henri Woltner, Chateau La Mission Haut Brion** 28 centre.